You Are a God Chaser If...

You Are a God Chaser If...

TOMMY TENNEY

Author's note: This book was written using direct quotes and adaptations from my book, *The God Chasers* (Shippensburg, PA; Destiny Image Publishers, 1998).

Destiny Image® Publishers, Inc.
P.O. Box 310
Shippensburg, PA 17257-0310

"Speaking to the Purposes of God for This Generation
and for the Generations to Come"

ISBN 0-7684-2164-0

For Worldwide Distribution
Printed in the U.S.A.

This book and all other Destiny Image, Revival Press, MercyPlace, Fresh Bread, Destiny Image Fiction, and Treasure House books are available at Christian bookstores and distributors worldwide.

For a U.S. bookstore nearest you, call **1-800-722-6774.**
For more information on foreign distributors, call **717-532-3040.**
Or reach us on the Internet:
www.destinyimage.com

You Are a God Chaser If...

YOU SEEK INTIMACY WITH GOD
OVER FLIRTING WITH GOD

You Are a God Chaser If...

ALL YOU WANT IS TO KNOW HIM.

We think we know where God lives.

We think we know what He likes, and we are *sure* we know what He dislikes.

We have studied God's Word and His old love letters to the churches so much that some of us claim to know *all* about God. But now people all around the world are beginning to hear a voice speak to them with persistent but piercing repetition in the stillness of the night:

"I'm not asking you how much you know *about* Me. I want to ask you, 'Do you really *know* Me? Do you really *want* Me?'"

Perhaps you too have heard this voice. I did, and it birthed a hunger in my heart that just wouldn't go away. I was a "professional preacher" and a successful evangelist, but felt a gnawing vacuum of emptiness in the midst of my ministry accomplishments. I was in a frustrating funk, a divine depression of destiny.

I am a fourth generation Spirit-filled Christian, three generations deep into ministry, but to be honest with you, I was sick of church. I was just like most of the people we try to lure into our services every week. They won't come because they are sick of church too. On the other hand, they're also *hungry for God*.

You are a God Chaser if you are hungry to hear from something that's beyond yourself, something you are not hearing in the Church of today! The bottom line is that you are sick of church because the Church has been somewhat less than what the Book advertised!

God Chasers seem to suffer from the same hunger pangs as people who had never met Jesus before! They aren't content just to know *about* Jesus anymore.

You can know all about presidents, royalties, and celebrities; you can know their eating habits, address, and marital status. But knowing about them doesn't imply intimacy. That doesn't mean you *know* them.

For too long the Church has been conversant only in the *things* of God. You're a God Chaser if you would rather talk *with* God than talk techniques about *serving* God or sharing information *about* Him. That's the difference between knowing someone and knowing about him.

It's simply not enough to know about God. We have churches filled with people who can win Bible trivia contests but who don't know Him. Mere knowledge about a person is not the same as an intimate friendship.

In all my reading and study of the Bible, I have never found any person mentioned in the Scriptures who really had a "God encounter" and then "backslid" and rebelled against God. Once you experience God in His glory, you can't turn away from Him or forget His touch. It's not just an argument or a doctrine; it's an *experience*. That is why the apostle Paul said, "...I know *whom* I have believed..." (2 Tim. 1:12). Unfortunately, many people in the Church would say, "I know *about* whom I have believed." That means they haven't met Him in His glory.

There is something in us that makes us afraid of the commitment that comes with real intimacy with God. For one thing, intimacy with God requires *purity*. The days of fun and games in the Church are over.

In other words, if your concept of "church" means low commitment, high anointing, the feeling of being blessed, and receiving the "spiritual gifts" like a religious "gold-digger," then all you've ever wanted to do is "date" God. However, the last time I checked, He was still looking for a *bride*, not a girlfriend; one who is willing to *put on the ring of commitment*.

You are a God Chaser if you are ready to commit to God? Are you ready to give up all the "fun and games" simply to know Him? God is saying to the Church today, "If you want to marry Me, let's do this right. Let's pledge ourselves to each other." We've chased after cheap thrills without the commitment, but God is saying "Intimacy." And *out of that intimacy* will come revival

There is so much more of God available than we have ever known or imagined, but we have become so satisfied with where we are and what we have that we don't press in for God's best. Yes, God is moving among us and working in our lives, but we have been content to comb the carpet for crumbs as opposed to having the abundant loaves of hot bread God has prepared for us in the ovens of Heaven! He has prepared a great table of His presence in this day, and He is calling to the Church, "Come and dine."

Let's not ignore God's summons while carefully counting our stale crumbs of yesteryear's bread. Millions of people outside our church walls are starving for life. They are sick and overstuffed with our man-made programs for self-help and self-advancement. They are starving for *Him*, not stories *about* Him. They want the food, but all we have to give them is a tattered menu vacuum-sealed in plastic to protect the fading images of what once was from the grasping fingers of the desperately hungry.

It should convict and shame the Church to see so many hurting and searching people turn to psychics, astrology, and spiritists for guidance and hope in their lives! People are so desperate for hope that they will accept canned script from paid marketers as spiritual insight. *Oh, the depth of spiritual hunger in the world!* There is only one reason so many people are so willing to attempt to get in touch with something from the other side, even accepting the counterfeit—they don't know where to find the real thing. The blame for that can only fall in one place: the Church.

Often we in the Church are so full and satisfied with other things that we insist on "getting by" with our crumbs of the past. We're happy with our music the way it is. We're happy with our "renewal" meetings. It is time for some of what I have politely termed "divine discontent." Can I say it? *I'm not happy.* By that I mean that even though I have been a participant in what some would call the revival of a lifetime, I am still not happy. Why? Because I know what *can* happen. I can catch Him. I know that there is far more than anything we have seen or hoped for yet, and it has become a holy obsession. I want God. I want more of Him.

Catching Him. Really, it's an impossible phrase. We can no more catch Him than the east can catch the west; they're too far removed from each other. It's like playing chase with my daughter. Often as she arrives home from a day of school, we play this little game that countless fathers and children play around the world. When she comes and tries to catch me, even with my hulking frame, I really don't have to run. I just artfully dodge this way and that, and she can't even touch me, because a six-year-old can't catch an adult. But that's not really the purpose of the game, because a few minutes into it, she laughingly says, "Oh daddy," and it's at that moment that she captures my heart, if not my presence or body. And then I turn and she's no longer chasing me, but I'm chasing her, and I catch her and we tumble in the grass with hugs and kisses. The pursuer becomes the pursued. So can we catch Him? Not really, but we can catch His heart. David did. And if we catch His heart, then He turns and chases us. That's the beauty of being a God Chaser. You're chasing the impossible, knowing it's possible.

YOU DON'T CARE ABOUT BEING "RELIGIOUSLY CORRECT."

Are you so hungry for God that it consumes you to the point where you couldn't care less what people think of you? I'm not talking about the excitement of praise and worship, as we would call it. I'm talking about a hunger for God's presence. Are you pursuing His presence?

I used to pursue preaching good sermons and great crowds and attempt great accomplishments for Him. But I've been ruined. Now I'm a God Chaser. Nothing else matters anymore. I couldn't care less about what other people or ministers think about me. I'm going after God. That's not a pride thing; it's a hunger thing. When you pursue God with all your heart, soul, and body, He will turn to meet you and you will come out of it *ruined* for the world.

Our problem is that we have never really been hungry. We have allowed things of this realm to satisfy our lives and satiate our hunger. We have come to God week after week, year after year, just to have Him fill in the little empty spaces. I tell you that God is tired of being "second place" to everything else in our lives. He is even tired of being second to the local church program and church life!

Everything good, including the things your local church does, should flow from the presence of God. Our primary motivating factor should be, "We do it because of Him and because it is His heart." But if we're not careful, we can get so caught up in doing things *for* Him that we forget about *Him.*

Good things have become the enemy of the best things. I challenge you to let your heart be broken by the Holy Ghost. It's time for you to make your life holy. Quit watching what you used to watch;

quit reading what you used to read if you are reading it more than you read His Word. He must be your first and greatest hunger.

Satan's ploy has been to keep us so full of junk that we're not hungry for Him, and it has worked magnificently for centuries. The enemy has made us so accustomed to surviving on an earthly prosperity but a beggar's subsistence in the spirit realm, that just a crumb of God's presence will satisfy. There are those who are not content with crumbs anymore. They want *Him*, and nothing else will do.

You are a God Chaser if you refuse to be content with anything less than *a full loaf*! Counterfeits no longer satisfy or interest you; you must have the *real thing.* Most of us, however, keep our lives so jammed with junk food for the soul and amusements for the flesh that we don't know what it is to be really hungry.

Have you ever seen hungry people? I mean *really hungry* people. If you could come with me on a ministry trip to Ethiopia or travel to some famine-ravaged land, you would see what happens when sacks of rice are brought out among *really hungry people*. They come from everywhere in a matter of seconds. Most of us eat before we go to a church meeting, so the sight of a loaf of bread on a church altar wouldn't do anything for us. But when God told me one morning to preach about the bread, He also said "Son, if they were physically starving, *they would act differently*."

The actions of *really hungry people* seem to match what Jesus said about the Kingdom of Heaven, "...*the violent take it by force*" (Mt. 11:12)! For some reason that doesn't sound like us, does it?

We've become so "churchified" that we have our own form of "political correctness" and polite etiquette. Since we don't want to be too radical, we line all the chairs up in nice rows and expect our services to conform to equally straight and regimented lines as well. We need to get so desperately hungry for Him that we *literally forget our manners*! The most apparent differecne between liturgical worship and "charismatic" worship is that one has a printed program and the other is memorized. (Worshipers in both "camps" are beginning to display a desperate hunger for God's presence!)

Everybody whom I can think of in the New Testament record who "forgot their manners" received something from Him. I'm not talking about rudeness for the sake of rudeness; I'm talking about rudeness born out of desperation! What about the desperate woman with an incurable hemorrhaging problem who elbowed and shoved her way through the crowd until she touched the hem of the Lord's garment? (See Matthew 9:20-22.) What about the impertinent Canaanite woman who just kept begging Jesus to deliver her daughter from demonization in Matthew 15:22-28? Even though Jesus insulted her when He said, "It is not meet to take the children's bread, and to cast it to dogs" (Mt. 15:26b), she persisted. And she was so rude, so abrupt, and so pushy (or was she simply so desperately hungry for bread) that she replied, "Truth, Lord: yet the dogs eat of the crumbs which fall from their masters' table" (Mt. 15:27).

To be honest, I'm hoping that God grips men and women in His Church and causes them to become so obsessed with the bread of His presence that they will not stop. Once that happens, they don't want just a "bless me" touch. They will want Him to show up in the place no matter how much it costs or how uncomfortable it may feel. They may sound and act rude, but they won't really care about man's opinion, only about God's opinion. It is accurate to say that the Church, by and large, doesn't really have a place for people like that.

We've become satisfied with church proceeding in the dim "normal and status quo" mode. I'm not happy with it being that way—I want more! I don't know about you, but every empty seat I see in a church building screams out to me, "Can't you put a hungry body in this seat?" It feeds my holy frustration, my divine discontent.

I believe that God is about to release the spirit of a "breaker" (see Mic. 2:13) to come and literally break the heavens open so that everybody can eat and feed at God's table. Before the heavens can open, though, the fountains of the deep must be broken. (See Genesis 1:8; 7:11.) It's time for some church, somewhere, to forget about trying to be a "politically correct church" and break open the heavens that the manna might fall and start feeding the spiritually hungry of the city! It's time that we punch a hole in the heavens and break through in hungry travail so the glory of God can begin to shine down on our cities.

The only thing that is going to turn the focus and favor of God toward us is our hunger. We must repent, reach for His face, and pray, "God, look at us, and we'll look to You."

God is everywhere, but *He doesn't turn His face and His favor everywhere*. That is why He tells us to seek His face. Yes, He is present with you every time you meet with other believers in a worship service, but how long has it been since your hunger caused you to crawl up in His lap, and like a child, to reach up and take the face of God to turn it toward you? Intimacy with Him! That is what God desires, and His face should be our highest focus.

YOU HUNGER FOR THE BREAD OF HIS PRESENCE.

The priority of God's presence has been lost in the modern Church. We're like bakeries that are open, but have no bread. And furthermore, we're not interested in selling bread. We just like the chit-chat that goes on around cold ovens and empty shelves. (That especially concerns me because Jesus called Himself the "Bread of Life" in John 6:35.)

According to the Bible, Naomi and her husband and two sons left home and moved to Moab because there was a famine in Bethlehem. The literal meaning of the Hebrew term, *Bethlehem*, is "house of bread," so Naomi's family left the *house of bread* because there was *no bread in the house*. It's simple, why do people leave the churches? There's no bread. There's no presence of God.

Naomi and her family have something in common with the people who leave or totally avoid our churches today—they left "that" place and went somewhere else to try to find bread. Why are people flocking to the bars, the clubs, and the psychics by the millions? They're just trying to get by; they are just trying to survive because the Church has failed them. They looked, or their parents and friends looked and reported, and the spiritual cupboard was bare. There was no presence in the pantry; just empty shelves and offices full of recipes for bread. But the oven was cold and dusty.

It's obvious why people hardly bow their heads when they come in our meetings and places of worship. They don't sense God's presence in our gatherings because it's just not there sufficiently enough to register on their gauges. This, in turn, creates another problem. When people get just a little touch of God mixed with a lot of something that is not God, it inoculates them against the real thing. Once they've been "inoculated" by a crumb of God's presence, then when we say, "God really is here"; they say, "No, I've been there, done that. I bought that T-shirt, and I didn't find Him; it really didn't work for me." The problem is that God was there all right, but not enough of Him! There was no undeniable, overwhelming sense of His manifest presence.

People have come to the House of Bread time and again only to find there was simply *too much of man and too little of God* there. I have news for you: The Almighty One is out to restore the sense of His awesome manifest presence in our lives and places of worship!

God is getting ready to break out in America, even if He has to bypass her stuffy churches to break out in the barrooms! We would be wise to remember that He has bypassed the religious elite before to dine with the poor, the profane, and the prostitutes. The Western Church, and the American Church in particular, has exported its programs about God all over the world, but it is time for us to learn that our programs are not progress. What we need is His presence. We need to decide that whatever it takes and wherever it comes from, we must have Him.

Naomi and her daughter-in-law, Ruth, decide to risk everything in their search for bread:

> *And Elimelech Naomi's husband died; and she was left, and her two sons.*
>
> *And they took them wives of the women of Moab; the name of the one was Orpah, and the name of the other Ruth: and they dwelled there about ten years.*
>
> *And Mahlon and Chilion died also both of them; and the woman was left of her two sons and her husband.*
>
> *Then she arose with her daughters in law, that she might return from the country of Moab: for **she had heard** in the country of*

> *Moab how that **the Lord had visited His people in giving them bread*** (Ruth 1:3-6).

When Bethlehem, the house of bread, is empty, people are forced to look elsewhere for the bread of life. The dilemma they face is that the world's alternatives can be deadly. As Naomi was to discover, Moab is a cruel place. Moab will steal your sons from you and bury them before their time. Moab will separate you from your spouse. Moab will rob the very vitality of life from you. In the end, all that Naomi had left were two daughters-in-law whom she had known only ten years. With nothing but a gloomy and disastrous future staring her in the face, she told them, "You might as well not hang around me either. I don't have any more sons to give you." But then she said, "I heard a rumor…." (See Ruth 1:6.)

There is an information "grapevine" that winds its way through every community, hamlet, and city of the world. It is the "grapevine of the hungry." If just one of them hears the rumor that there is bread back in the House of Bread, the news will flow like a surge of electricity through a power line at near the speed of light. The news of bread will leapfrog from one household to the other, from one place to another almost instantaneously. You won't have to worry about advertising on TV or promoting it in the usual ways of the world. The hungry will just hear.

When that happens, we won't be able to hold them in our buildings, no matter how many services we conduct each day. Why? How? *All you must do is get the bread back!*

Now, today, there is a faint rumor that there is bread in God's house once again. This generation, like Ruth (a picture of the unchurched unsaved), is about to sidle up to Naomi (a picture of a prodigal) to say, "If you heard there is really bread there, then I'm going with you. Wherever you go, I'll go. Your people will be my people, and your God will be my God" (see Ruth 1:16). *If...there's really* bread. So tattered was the reputation of Bethlehem (the house of bread) that Orpah didn't go. How many like her "don't go" because the history of hype from the Church exhausts their energy? They can't make the trip.

Do you know what will instantly integrate someone directly into the fabric of the local church? It will happen the moment they taste *the bread of His presence in that place*. When Naomi heard that there was bread back in Bethlehem, she rose from her sorrow to go to the house of bread.

Two things happen when the bread of God's presence is restored to the Church. Naomi was a prodigal who left the house of bread when that table became bare. Yet once she heard that God had restored bread to Bethlehem, the house of bread, she quickly returned. *The prodigals will come walking back into Bethlehem* from Moab once they know there is bread in the house, and *they won't come alone*. Naomi came back to the house of bread accompanied by Ruth, who had never been there before. The never saved will come. As a result, Ruth became part of the Messianic lineage of Jesus when she married Boaz and bore him a son named Obed, who was the father of Jesse, the father of David. (See Ruth 4:17.) Future royalty awaits our hunger-spurred actions.

If God really shows His "face" in your church, I can assure you that the "grapevine of the hungry" in your city or region will spread the news overnight! Before you can even pry the doors open the next day, the hungry will come and stand in line for fresh bread. Why don't we see that kind of response now? The hungry have been "burned." As soon as the tiniest trickle of God's presence flows through our services, we want to tell the whole world, "There's a river of God's anointing that has broken out over here."

We falsely advertise and hype-up our claims that there is bread in our house. But when the hungry come, all they can do is scrounge through the carpet for a few crumbs of yesteryear's revivals. We talk grandly about where He has been and what He has done, but we can say very little about what He is doing among us today. That isn't God's fault; it is ours. We have only remnants of what used to be—a residue of the fading glory. And unfortunately, we keep the veil of secrecy over that fact. We camouflage our emptiness like the priesthood in Jesus' day kept the veil in place with no ark of the covenant behind it.

God may have to "pierce" the veil of our flesh to reveal our (the Church's) inner emptiness also. It's a pride problem—we point with pride to where He has been (protecting the temple tradition) while we deny the obviously apparent "glory" of the Son of God. The religious spirits of Jesus' day didn't want the populace to realize that there was no glory behind their veil. Jesus' presence presented problems.

Religious spirits must preserve where He's been at the expense of where He is!

But a man with an experience is never at the mercy of a man with only an argument. If we can lead people into the manifest presence of God, all false theological houses of cards will tumble down. They will have tasted the fresh bread of His presence.

You are a God Chaser if you will do whatever it takes to produce hot loaves of fresh bread!

YOU DESIRE HABITATION, NOT VISITATION.

Do you seek God for what He can give, or just because you want *Him*? God is not coming to people who merely seek His benefits. He's coming to people who seek His face. However, the only way He will turn His visitation in revival into habitation for life is if you and I will prepare a place for Him with tears and repentance.

God is looking for someone who is willing to tie a rope around an ankle (the same way the chief priests did in the Old Testament) and say, "If I perish, I perish; but I am going to see the king. I want to do everything I can to go behind that veil. I'm going to put on the blood, I'm going to repent, I'm going to do everything

I can because I'm tired of knowing about Him. I want to know Him. I've got to see His face."

When God tells us, "You can't see My face," most of us are satisfied that we've done our religious duty and we quickly return to life as usual. Moses, however, persisted. He had learned that it isn't impertinent to pursue God for His own sake; it is God's greatest desire.

> *And [Moses] said, I beseech Thee, show me Thy glory.*
>
> *And He said, I will make all My goodness pass before thee, and I will proclaim the name of the Lord before thee; and will be gracious to whom I will be gracious, and will show mercy on whom I will show mercy.*
>
> *And He said, **Thou canst not see My face: for there shall no man see Me, and live.***
>
> *And the Lord said, Behold, there is a place by Me, and thou shalt stand upon a rock:*

> *And it shall come to pass, while My glory passeth by, that I will put thee in a clift of the rock, and will cover thee with My hand while I pass by:*
>
> *And I will take away Mine hand, and thou shalt see My back parts: but **My face shall not be seen*** (Exodus 33:18-23).

It would have been easy for this man to have been satisfied with God's first answer, but he wasn't. Moses wasn't selfish or presumptuous. He wasn't seeking material things or personal fame. He wasn't even seeking miracles or gifts (and Paul even instructed us to seek after the best gifts in his letter to the Corinthians). Moses simply wanted God, and that is the greatest gift and blessing we can ever give Him. Yet Moses had to pursue Him, and it didn't come easy.

While Moses pursued God on a mountaintop on the Israelites' behalf, his brother Aaron, the high priest, yielded to the pressure of public opinion and agreed to make an idolatrous golden calf for the Israelites. Then the people pursued their pleasures in the valley while Moses watched the finger of God inscribe the law onto tablets of stone. It was after this episode that God told Moses He would still allow the Israelites to cross over into the promised land, but they would have to make do with an angel, "...for I will not go up in the midst of thee; for thou art a stiffnecked people: lest I consume thee in the way" (Ex. 33:3).

Most of us would have leaped at the chance to have the verbal strength and promise of God to go with us wherever we go. But who is to say we even know where we should go? Moses wisely answered, "If You don't lead, I'm not going anywhere." *He understood that it was "good" to have God go with you, but that it was "better" to go with God.*

God negotiated with Moses, "I will give thee rest" (Ex. 33:14). I think the New Testament fulfillment of God's "rest" to the Church is found in the supernatural gifts of the Spirit that enable us to effectively train and minister to the Body with a minimum of human effort. In Isaiah 28:11-12 the Scriptures say, "For with stammering lips and another tongue will He speak to this people. To whom He said, This is the rest...." I believe that the gifts of the Spirit (including tongues) are the "rest" referred to here. God was saying metaphorically, "Moses, I'll give you the gifts, the 'rest,' " and Moses was saying, "I don't want the gifts; *I want You.*"

The Church is so enamored with the gifts of the Spirit that we don't know the Giver of the gifts. We're having so much fun playing with God's gifts that we've even forgotten to thank Him. The best thing we can do as God's kids is to lay down His gifts long enough to go sit in the Father's lap. We must seek the Giver, not the gifts! We must seek His face, not His hands!

The Israelites rarely took time to thank God for His mighty acts because they were too busy compiling "want lists" and official complaints connected with their physical and personal desires. The vast majority of us today have done the same thing.

Moses, however, wanted something more. He had experienced the miracles. He had heard God's voice and witnessed His delivering power. More than any other person alive at that time, Moses had even experienced the manifest presence of God in measure, in temporary visitation. But everything he saw and experienced in God told him that there was *far more* just waiting for him beyond the cloud. He longed for more than *visitation*; his soul longed for *habitation*. He wanted more than just seeing God's finger or hearing His voice speaking from a cloud or a burning bush. He had gone beyond fear to love, and God's abiding presence had become his consuming desire. That is why he begged God in Exodus 33:18: "I beseech Thee, *show me Thy glory*."

He wanted to see God's face!

The bottom line is this: If you are really hungry to see Daddy come on the scene, then you have to understand that you must stop seeking His benefits and quit asking for Him to do this and that. We have managed to turn what we erroneously call "church" into a big "bless me club" where we sign up for this blessing and that blessing. I'm not so sure that we need to seek blessings anymore. That's what the Israelites did in all the centuries after they ran from the face of God. We need to seek brokenness and repentance, and say by our actions as well as our words, "God, we want You. We don't care if You 'do' anything or not. We are crawling up on the altar. Let Your fire of cleansing fall so we can finally see Your face."

We are too easily satisfied with things that are not quite what they ought to be. I'm pressing my point because the Church is in grave danger of once again stopping at the "burning bush" in this wonderful visitation of God's presence. There is a greater purpose behind the meetings taking place around the world (and it isn't just for us to get blessed). God wants to break open the heavens over our cities *so the people who are without God will know that He is Lord and that He loves them.* Now that is the true purpose of God's visitation among men. We need to get our eyes off the toys and onto the purpose.

You need to forget who's around you and abandon the "normal protocol." God is in the business of re-defining what we call "church" anyway. He's looking for people who are hot after His heart. He wants a Church of Davids who are after His own heart (not just His hand). (See Acts 13:22.) You can seek His blessing and play with His toys, or you can say, "No, Daddy, I don't just want the blessings; I want *You.* I want You to come close. I want You to touch my eyes, touch my heart, touch my ears, and change me, Lord. I'm tired of me the way I am, because if I can change, then the cities can change too." Habitation!

YOU HAVE MOVED
FROM DANCING AT THE VEIL
TO LIVING WITHIN THE VEIL

You Choose Intimate Relationship Over Distant Respect.

The Church today has made it to the halfway point in its journey across the wilderness. We are camped at the foot of Mount Sinai, much like the children of Israel in the Book of Exodus. It is obvious that we have reached the point where we are going to have to make a decision. Will we go in or run away?

The Lord brought the descendants of Abraham to the base of Mount Sinai, but it wasn't easy. When the multitude of people needed food, God wanted them to seek Him for their bread, but instead they berated Moses and talked about how good it was back in Egypt, the place of their bondage. The same thing happened when there was a water shortage.

Instead of asking God or believing in His abundant supply, they immediately cornered Moses to complain and talk about the "good old days" in Egypt. God had something better for the children of Israel, but it was almost as if He was thinking, *If I can just get them past this mountain, then I can have hope of taking them all the way.*

The sad and unfortunate truth of the Book of Exodus is that the motley group of people God brought to Mount Sinai was *not the group of people* that He took across the river Jordan into the promised land. *Something happened at the mountain.* God called them and made them a nation for the first time in their history. He called them to a place—a place of blessing and a place of change—and they didn't want to go.

Don't fall into the trap of thinking that this "place" was merely some physical spot on the map, because these people were already traipsing across the wilderness. Their blessing didn't consist of some rocky real estate someplace, although the promised land was part of the package deal. God called them to *a promised place in Him.* He called them to a place of covenant, a place of intimacy with their Creator that was not offered to any other people on the planet at that time. *That's the secret of the secret place.* We think that the idea of a "kingdom of priests" is an exclusively New Testament or Christian idea, but it was also God's original plan for Israel! (See Exodus 19:3-6.)

Although the first generation of Israelites gathered around the mountain would ultimately believe the fearful spies and shrink away from the promised land in fear, the real cause of their failure is found right there at the foot of Mount Sinai. God intended for *all* the Israelites to *come close to Him* on the mountain, but they were uncomfortable.

> *And all the people saw the thunderings, and the lightnings, and the noise of the trumpet, and the mountain smoking: and*

*when the people saw it, **they removed, and stood afar off.***

*And they said unto Moses, Speak thou with us, and we will hear: but **let not God speak with us, lest we die.***

And Moses said unto the people, Fear not: for God is come to prove you, and that His fear may be before your faces, that ye sin not.

*And **the people stood afar off**, and **Moses drew near** unto the thick darkness where God was* (Exodus 20:18-21).

They saw the lightning and heard the thunder, and they shrank back in fear. They ran from His presence instead of pursuing Him as Moses did. They were unhappy with the style of leadership that God had chosen. (He couldn't lay down His identity as the Almighty God just to please man then, and He won't do it today either.) So the end result of their flight from holy intimacy that day was that they died before they or their children ever entered the promised land. They preferred *distant respect over intimate relationship*.

It wasn't God's original plan for the first generation of Israelites to die in the wilderness. He wanted to take the same group of people whom He brought out of the land of bondage into the land of promise. He wanted to give His new nation of former slaves their very own land and inheritance, but they wouldn't have it because of fear and unbelief. Their doom was sealed when they looked across the Jordan at the promised land and shrank back, but it really began when they shrank back from God's presence in the cloud on Mount Sinai. It was there that they ran from God and demanded that Moses stand between them.

The Church has been suffering from the same problem ever since. We often prefer that a man stand between us and God. We have a hell-inspired, fleshly fear of holy intimacy with God. The roots of this fear reach all the way back to the Garden of Eden. Adam and Eve hid in shameful fear while God longed for sweet fellowship.

Now we face the same challenge as the children of Israel thousands of years ago: *Do we run away or go in?* Into what? Into His presence.

God was calling the people to intimacy and they ran the other way! They told Moses, "...let not God speak with us, lest we die" (Ex. 20:19). They understood that only things that match the character of God as depicted in the Ten Commandments could stand to live in His presence. By running away, they were saying, "Look, we don't want to live up to that. Don't let God talk to us right now." All God wanted them to do when He gave Moses the Ten Commandments was to clean up their act so He could do more than just see them from a distance. He wanted to walk with them once again in the cool of the desert day. He wanted to sit with them and share His heart in intimate communion. Nothing has changed, my friend. He wants to do the same thing now with you and me. Our proper response is, "Please, God, speak with us *even if we have to die!*"

I believe the Church stands at a critical cross-roads today. On the one hand, we could say, "We've come too far to turn around now." But we also could say, "We're really tired. We want to sit here for a while." The real question is, "What does God say?" I believe He wants us to grasp where we are at this point. He wants us to reach out and receive everything He has to give us for today.

You and I are going to do one of two things from this point on:

1. We will grow into a relationship with Him, no matter what it costs us, or,

2. We will turn back to where we came from and become a program-driven, meeting-going, organizing, committee-run church people, doing all the "good" things that "good people" are supposed to

do. We will end up fondly looking back on this time of decision and saying, "Those were the days."

I don't know about you, but I don't want to grow old and look back with regret someday and say, "Oh, those were great days." Why should I when I've come to understand that with God I can live in the present tense? I can walk in the freshness of what He has for me every day. If we dare to follow God today, then on some tomorrow we may be able to look back and say, "I remember those years; that was before we had the great revival of His presence!"

Frankly, our future depends on our outlook in this hour of decision. If our outlook is, "Well, we've done pretty well," then this is probably all we'll do. But our futures will look totally different if we say, "Thank You, Lord…but where's the rest? There's got to be more! Show me Your glory!"

We need to learn from the events at Mount Sinai. First of all, God revealed on Mount Sinai that

He wanted to begin dealing with the people *directly* and personally. Until that day, Moses had always relayed to the Israelites everything that God said. That was a time of transition, a period in which God was saying, "Okay, it's time to grow up. I want to talk to you directly from now on as an entire nation of holy priests. I don't want to have any more intermediaries. I love Moses, but I don't want to have to speak through him to reach you. I want to deal with you directly as My nation, as My people."

Unfortunately, the Israelites suffered from the same problem many Christians do today. We have become addicted to the anointing, the relayed word of good preaching and teaching. Too many of us have become "milk babies" who want to sit on padded pews in an air-conditioned and climate-controlled building where someone else will pre-digest what God has to say and then regurgitate it back to us in a half-digested form.

The solution is hunger and desperation for God Himself without intermediaries. We need to pray, "God, I'm tired of everybody else hearing from You! Where is the lock on my prayer closet? I'm going to lock myself away until I hear from You for myself!"

God is tired of having *long distance relationships* with His people. He was tired of it thousands of years ago in Moses' day, and He is tired of it today. He really wants to have intimate, close encounters with you and me. He wants to invade our homes with His abiding presence in a way that will make every visitor begin to weep with wonder and worship the moment they enter.

As far as I can tell, there is only one thing that stops Him. He is not going to come where He doesn't find hunger. He looks for the hungry. Hunger means you're dissatisfied with the way it has been because it forced you to live without Him in His fullness. He only comes when you are ready to turn it all over to Him. God is coming back to repossess His Church, but you have to be hungry. How hungry are you?

YOU REFUSE TO TAKE SHORTCUTS

TO HIS PRESENCE

you desire His presence at all costs.

Do you really know what you are asking for when we you say you "want God"? I know I thought I did, but I didn't. Believe me, when God actually shows up, you won't be prepared for the reality of His presence.

I had often read of Isaiah's encounter with the presence of God, and even dared dream I might experience myself.

> *In the year that king Uzziah died I saw also the Lord sitting upon a throne, high and lifted up, and His train filled the temple.*
>
> *Above it stood the seraphims: each one had six wings; with twain he covered his face,*

> *and with twain he covered his feet, and with twain he did fly.*
>
> *And one cried unto another, and said, Holy, holy, holy, is the Lord of hosts: the whole earth is full of His glory.*
>
> *And the posts of the door moved at the voice of him that cried, and the house was filled with smoke* (Isaiah 6:1-4).

I'd never understood what it meant for the glory of the Lord to fill a place. I had sensed God come in places, I had sensed Him come by, but one Sunday morning at the church of a pastor friend, even after there was all of God that I thought was available in the building, more of His presence literally packed itself into the room. It was like the bridal train of a bride that, after she has personally entered the building, continues to enter the building after her. God was there; of that there was no doubt.

But more of Him kept coming in the place until, as in Isaiah 6, it literally filled the building.

Primarily one thing happened that day: The presence of God showed up. When that happens, the first thing you do is the same thing Isaiah did when he saw the Lord high and lifted up. He cried out from the depths of his soul:

> *Then said I, Woe is me! for I am undone; because I am a man of unclean lips, and I dwell in the midst of a people of unclean lips: for mine eyes have seen the King, the Lord of hosts* (Isaiah 6:5).

You see, the instant Isaiah the prophet, the chosen servant of God, saw the King of glory, what he used to think was clean and holy now looked like filthy rags. He was thinking, *I thought I knew God, but I didn't know **this much** of God!*

God came so suddenly and so forcefully into the building that Sunday that we were afraid to do anything unless He specifically told us to do it. His presence had always been there of course, but not the weighty manifest presence we experienced that morning. In those moments, all we could do was sit there, trembling. We even were afraid to take an offering without specific permission from God!

The thick blanket of His tangible presence was so heavy that I received an "up close and personal" understanding of what is meant by God's Word when it says:

> *And it came to pass, when the priests were come out of the holy place, that the cloud filled the house of the Lord,*
>
> *So that the priests could not stand to minister because of the cloud: for the glory of the Lord had filled the house of the Lord* (1 Kings 8:10-11).

I now know why the high priests of old would say to their fellow priests, "Tie a rope around my ankle, because I'm going into the place where the glory of God abides. I've done everything I know to make myself ready, but I am in awe of God." Personally, I'm not afraid of God; I love Him. But I now have a respect for the glory and the holy things of God that I confess I didn't have before.

It used to be easy to handle the anointing, but now I know it is a sacred thing.

David learned the same thing when he and his crew tried to transport the ark of the covenant from Abinadab's house to Jerusalem.

> *And they set the ark of God upon a new cart, and brought it out of the house of Abinadab that was in Gibeah: and Uzzah and Ahio, the sons of Abinadab, drave the new cart....*
>
> *And when they came to Nachon's threshingfloor, Uzzah put forth his hand to the ark of God, and took hold of it; for the oxen shook it.*

> *And the anger of the Lord was kindled against Uzzah; and God smote him there for his error; and there he died by the ark of God.* (2 Samuel 6:3,6-7)

David and his troupe were trying to handle the holy presence and glory of God with human hands. How do you handle the holiness and glory of God? God will only let you do things your way just so far. David's problems came when he and his group tried to continue on as normal past God's "speed bump." The Lord never intended for His glory to creak along on the back of man's mechanisms, vehicles, or programs. He has always ordained for His glory to be transported by sanctified or set apart holy human vessels who reverence and respect His holiness.

When David's procession came to God's holy shaking place in the road, the oxen stumbled and Uzzah reached out to steady the ark. God's glory "broke out" on the flesh that drew near to it in a living state and Uzzah was instantly killed. *Only dead men can see God's face, and only repentant dead flesh can touch His glory.*

David had been doing everything he knew to do in the most respectable manner that he knew of. He and his procession were a happy little "church" taking the presence of God to the place where it belonged. Then they hit a holy bump in the road at the threshing floor of Nachon. When Uzzah casually reached out to steady "God's box" from falling off of man's vehicle, God seemed to say, "Look, I've let you come this far in your own manner; enough is enough. If you really want My presence back in Jerusalem, then you're going to have to do it My way." God broke out of His box and caused man's plans to fall that day, and it would take David three months to recover, repent, research, and return for God's glory.

The same thing happens today when we encounter God's manifest glory. Too often we reach out in fleshly presumption to stop the God we've carefully contained in a box from falling off of our rickety man-made ministry program or tradition. We shouldn't be surprised when God's glory breaks out of our doctrinal or traditional boxes and shocks us. *Something always dies when God's glory encounters living flesh.*

David changed his plans and methods because the weightiness of the presence of God suddenly dawned on him. He began to think, *This is no small matter. What are we doing? Am I really the one who should be doing this?*

That is exactly where the Church is at this crucial moment in time: We have reached the point where we are trying to transport the glory back to where it belongs. We've run into the shaking place at God's threshing floor and it is time to ask ourselves, "Are we really the ones? Do we really want to do it? Are we willing to pay the price and obey God's voice at all costs? Are we willing to learn anew how to handle the holy things of God?"

It's when you hit that holy bump that you realize, "This won't work anymore. This is not right anymore." Until you hit that bump, you will probably be perfectly satisfied and at ease with a little dancing, some small harps (that aren't too noisy), a few people singing and dancing, and maybe even a few less conservative things from time to time. But once you decide to return God's glory to its proper place, you are destined to hit a holy bump where *God's glory will appear and slay some flesh* right in front of everybody. True repentance is an awesome flesh-death sight to behold...too much for some to stomach and too high of price for some to pay.

Have you counted the cost? You are a God Chaser if you want His glory at all costs!

YOU SEEK WORSHIP

OVER ENTERTAINMENT

ALL YOU WANT TO DO IS WORSHIP HIM.

I was launched on this journey when God spoke to me and said, "Son, the services that you consider your favorite services and those I favor are not the same services." That is when I realized that we often come to church to "get something" from God, when the Bible tells us over and over again to "minister *unto the Lord*." Yes, we're involved in ministry all right. Our lives are so filled with ministry to people and the needs of people that we very seldom enter into a place where we can minister to Him. We go away week after week self-gratified, with our itches scratched and our narrow personal needs met.

When will we hear God's still small voice saying, "Would somebody just love *Me*?"

We need to return to the simplicity of our childhood in our relationship with the heavenly Father. Every night that I'm home, I rock my six-year-old daughter to sleep because I love her. Usually she will lay back in my arms, and just before she drifts off to sleep she will remember the problems of the day and say something like, "Daddy, this little boy was mean to me on the playground at school," or "Daddy, I had trouble on my spelling test today." To her these seem like giant problems. I always try to reassure her that everything will be all right in those moments because she is resting in my arms and because I love her. It doesn't matter what anyone said on the playground, and none of her little failures have any power to hurt her because she is in my arms.

Somehow, when I'm able to weave my way through the labyrinth of a six-year-old mind and bring peace to her, I get to enjoy my favorite part of the day. That is when my little girl just lays her head back to look at me with her eyes half open and give me her little smile. The only way I know to describe it is that her face displays sheer adoration and complete security in those moments. She doesn't have to speak; I understand. And then in complete peace she drifts off to sleep, with the smile of safety and trust on her face.

God wants us to do the same thing. Too often we come to Him at the end of our day and "worship" Him with premanufactured mechanics and memorized words. Then, since we are almost totally absorbed with our "playground" offenses and the temporal problems of the day, we lay back in His presence just long enough to say our string of words and deliver our wish list. Then we jump up and run off to continue our frustrated rat-race lives. Often we never seem to find that place of perfect peace.

What He wants us to do is just look at Him. Yes, we can tell Him what we feel. We need to tell Him, but He is really waiting to receive our most intimate worship and adoration, the kind that transcends mere words or outward actions. Unfortunately, all too often *we want God present in our services but refuse* (or ignore) *to worship Him* as we should.

For too long, the Church has asked God to be "present" but never placed His presence in a position of honor. That means that what we really wanted were His "tricks." We wanted His divine healings, supernatural giftings, and all the miraculous things He can do; but we really didn't want to honor Him. How can I say such a thing? Ask yourself if most of our church services have been custom-tailored to entertain people or God. Is it more important to us that when an influential man or woman leaves, he or she says, "Oh, that was good. I enjoyed that"; or that God says, "Oh, that was good. I enjoyed that"?

If Heaven has a hall of fame, then I can tell you someone whose name is going to be right at the top of the list. It is Mary, the woman with the alabaster box. Remember her story? She wept over Jesus' feet and wiped them with her hair while He was reclining for a meal at a Pharisee's house. *The disciples were so embarrassed by the woman's actions that they wanted to throw her out*, but Jesus made her actions an eternal monument of selfless worship! Jesus didn't intervene because of Mary's talent, beauty, or religious achievements; He stepped in because of her worship. The disciples said, "To what purpose is this waste?" (Mt. 26:8b) Jesus said, "It's not waste; it's worship." Such worshipers must often ignore the stares and comments of a politically correct church while ministering to Jesus.

He desires our adoration and worship. Heaven's "hall of fame" is filled with the names of obscure people like the one leper who returned to thank God while nine never bothered. It will be filled with the names of people who so touched the heart and mind of God that He says, "I remember you. I know about you. Well done, My good and faithful servant."

Often I see the aisles of churches strewn with people who have climbed into the lap of the Father. I see them hiding their faces underneath benches and pews as they seek the face of God. Something is happening in the Church today, and it has nothing to do with the hype and manipulation of man. Aren't you sick of all that? Aren't you hungry for an encounter with God that's not contaminated by the vain promotions and manipulations of fleshly leaders? Don't you long to have God just introduce Himself to you?

Now, you can always count on some Pharisees with the leprosy of hypocrisy showing up to look with disdain as you rush in to throw your best at the Lord's feet, but who cares? Who knows what problems will be lifted from your shoulders in that moment? Who knows what worries, fears, and anxieties will fade away when you hear Him say, "I accept you."

In God's eyes, we are all lepers in the spirit realm. We need to be those who return to the One who delivered us to offer thanksgiving. God's acceptance means you can ignore all the other voices that say, "I reject you." I don't mean to be rude, but who cares how many other lepers reject you when you have been healed and accepted by the King?

You may be only a few spiritual inches away from the encounter of a lifetime. If you want to see the face of God, then just follow Mary to the feet of Jesus. Pull out your alabaster box of precious sacrificial praise and worship. You've been holding your treasure back for too long, but there is One here who is worthy of it all. Don't hold anything back! Just worship Him.

YOU ARE A WALKING DEAD MAN

YOU'RE LOOKING FOR "OUT-OF-CONTROL" REVIVAL!

We don't understand revival; in fact, we don't even have the slightest concept of what true revival is. For generations we have thought of revival in terms of a banner across the road or over a church entryway. We think revival means a silver-tongued preacher, some good music, and a few folks who decide they're going to join the church. No! Real revival is when people are eating at a restaurant or walking through the mall when they suddenly begin to weep and turn to their friends and say, "I don't know what's wrong with me, but I know I've got to get right with God."

Real revival is when the most "difficult" and unreachable person you know comes to Jesus against all odds and possibilities. Frankly, the main reason such people aren't reached any other time is because they are seeing *too little of God and too much of man*. People don't want doctrine, they don't want tracts, and they don't want our feeble arguments; they just want *Him*!

God wants to reveal Himself among us. He wants to come ever stronger, and stronger, and stronger, and stronger until your flesh won't be able to stand it. The beauty of it is this: neither will the unsaved who are driving by be able to resist. It's beginning to happen. I have seen the day when sinners veer off the highway when they drive by places of an open heaven. They pull into parking lots with puzzled looks, and they knock on the doors and say, "*Please, there's something here…I've got to have it.*"

Aren't you tired of trying to pass out tracts, knock on doors, and make things happen? We've been trying to make things happen for a long time. Now *He* wants to make it happen!

I am weary of trying to accomplish God's works with the hands of man. What we need for nation-wide revival is one thing and one thing only: We need to have God show up.

If you want your local high school classes to turn into prayer meetings, then you will need to see God show up. I'm not talking about a theoretical or historical occurrence. There have been times recently when God's glory has been flowing in His churches so much that His people had to be careful in area restaurants. Simply bowing their heads to pray over their meal, they look up to see waitresses and other customers all around, just weeping uncon-trollably and saying, *"What is it with you people?"*

My wife was standing in line to pay for some purchases at a store when a lady tapped her on the shoulder. She turned around to see who it was to find a total stranger weeping unashamedly. This lady told my wife, "I don't know where you've been, and I don't know what you've got. But my husband is a lawyer and I'm in the middle of a divorce." She began to blurt out her other problems and finally said, "What I'm really saying is, I need God."

My wife looked around and said, "You mean right here?"

She said, "Right here."

My wife just had to ask again, "Well, what about the people in line?"

Suddenly the lady turned to the woman standing in line behind her and said, "Ma'am, is it okay if I pray with this lady right here?"

But that lady was also crying and she said, "Yes, and pray with me too."

Most of what we have seen so far is the renewal of the Church. I'm thinking that revival is not the best word for what we are seeing because it refers to something that is dead being brought back to life. I don't have the terminology to describe what God is about to do. How do you describe a "tsunami"?

How do you describe a tidal wave? How do you talk about what God can do, along with the unspeakable grace and strength that come with it?

Unfortunately, most of the times we shout, "God is here!" the hungry come only to find that we have hyped and manipulated, and over-promoted and under-produced our goods. We've falsely portrayed every trickle of God's anointing as a mighty river, and to their dismay the only river they have found among us is a river of words. We sometimes even build magnificent bridges over dry riverbeds!

We can't expect the lost and the hurting to come running to our "river" only to discover that there's barely enough for them to get a single sip from God's glass. We've told them, "God is really here; there's food on the table," but every time they have believed our report, they have been forced to comb through the carpet for the mere crumbs of the promised feast.

Revival as we know it now is really the "recycling" of saved people through the Church to keep them fired up. But the next wave of true revival will bring waves of unchurched people into the House of Bread—people who have never darkened the door of a church in their lives. When they hear that there really is bread in the house, they will stream through our doors after smelling the fragrance of hot bread from the ovens of Heaven!

The biblical model I desire and dream of is God's dealings with the city of Ninevah. I want to see a wave of God sweep through a city, pushing before it all of man's arrogance while leaving behind it nothing but a trail of broken repentance. I'm hungry for revival like we see in Jonah's description of citywide repentance and fasting in Ninevah.

I don't care what a city or a thing or a person looks like; only God knows His plans for the future. Many Christians have written off major metropolitan cities such as Los Angeles, New York, Detroit, Chicago, or Houston. Los Angeles may be the home of thousands of pornographic places and the Hollywood film industry, but Ninevah was an even more unlikely place for revival in its day! To say nothing of Shanghai, New Delhi, Calcutta, Rio de Janeiro…and the list grows! But if someone can find the light switch, His glory will flood these cities. It must, because He said that the glory of God will cover the earth! (See Numbers 14:21.)

My definition of revival is when God's glory breaks out of the four walls of our churches to flow through the streets of the city. Revival of historical proportions in modern times would be when God invades the shopping malls on Friday night. I want to see every mall association be forced to hire full-time chaplains just to handle the crowds of people they find weeping under conviction each shopping day. I want to see citywide calls for volunteer ministers just to handle the flood of people who get convicted of their sins when they pass through the town. (Security guards know what to do with shop-lifters, but would they know what to do with people who come up to them in distress because they've been convicted of their sin?) Hasten the day!

The anointing and power of God's presence are going to come upon us so strongly that His presence will literally go before us into our offices, plants, prisons, and shopping malls. Because this great revival is based on His glory and presence and not on the works of man, it cannot be contained within the four walls of churches. God's glory must flow out to the world.

Before the real revival breaks out in the malls, it will have to break out in our church altars. Then it must spread to the back pews. Then through the threshold of the door and out into the streets!

When you read Ezekiel 47, isn't it ironic that the river of God's presence flowing from His sanctuary actually grew deeper the further away the prophet walked? Finally Ezekiel ended up in water that was over his head and he couldn't touch bottom. He was out of control. I am after an "out-of-control" revival! Its shallowest point should be at the "church" building!

Given the fact that water always seeks the lowest level and the path of least resistance, it is easy to see why Jesus, the "brightness of [the Father's] glory, and the express image of His person" (Heb. 1:3a), said, "...the poor have the gospel preached to them" (Mt. 11:5). *God's glory always seeks to fill the void in the lives of men*. In the days to come, God's glory will emanate from the most confounding places and individuals, and it will begin to flow and fill the lowest and most open of people. And He alone will receive the glory.

YOU CHOOSE TO ENTER HIS
PRESENCE RATHER THAN RUN
FROM HIS PRESENCE

YOU WILL BE BROKEN TO RECEIVE A BREAKTHROUGH.

If there has ever been a country ripe for revival, it is the United States. Wouldn't you agree? And if you do, are you willing to do something about it? You see, true revival will come only one way. It comes only when the priest and the ministers weep between the porch and the altar and cry out to Jesus Christ, "Spare the people." There is no shortcut to revival or the coming of His presence. God's glory only comes when repentance and brokenness drive you to your knees, because His presence requires purity. Only dead men see God's face. We cannot expect others to repent at that depth if you and I are not willing to continually walk in that level of repentance.

God cannot pass by the prayers of the broken-hearted and contrite who seek His face. When the full measure of the gathered prayers of God's people finally reach a crescendoing echo in God's ears, then it becomes too much for Him to wait any longer. The day will come when God says from His throne on high, "That's it."

I believe that when the conglomerate prayers of God's people gather together and finally reach a crescendo of power, hunger, and intensity, it finally gets to be "too much" for God to delay any longer. At that point He finally says, "That's it. I won't wait any longer. It is time!"

We are really praying for an opening in the heavens over our cities and our nation so that when the glory of God comes, the people in our area can't resist anymore because the stronghold of demonic powers is broken. How does that happen? It happens through a visitation of the manifestation of the glory of God. Oh, that "prayers" would arise that would both close the gates of hell and open the windows of Heaven!

I must warn you that sometimes you will be broken to get a breakthrough. It's just the way it happens. I encourage you to linger and soak in the presence of the Lord at every opportunity. When you draw near to Him, don't hurry and don't rush. Realize that this is (or should be) at the top of your priority list. Let God do a deep work in your heart and life. The purpose of His presence is to bring deliverance to the captives and victory to the children.

The Lord knows that we have tried to pave the way for people to come to God through painless, cheap grace and costless revival. But all we wound up with was bargain basement salvations that hardly lasted a week. Why? Because all we gave people was an emotional encounter with man when what they really needed was a flesh-death encounter with the glory and presence of God Himself.

I don't know about you, but I am tired of just being "another somebody" to the lost around me. I have made a decision. I made up my mind and set my heart to declare, "I am going to pursue the presence of God in my life. I am going to get so close to God that when I walk into secular and public places, people will meet Him." They may not know that I'm there, but they will definitely know that *He* is there. I want to be so saturated with God's presence that when I take a seat on a plane, then everyone near me will suddenly feel uncomfortable if they're not right with God—even though I haven't said a word. I'm not wanting to condemn or to convict them; I just want to carry the fragrance of my Father with me.

Will you join with me?

You Are a God Chaser If...

YOU PRESS IN AND LET GOD BREAK OUT!

For too long we only have allowed the Holy Spirit to take control *up to a certain point*. Basically, whenever things get outside of our comfort zone or just a little beyond our control, we pull in the reins (the Bible calls it "quenching the Spirit" in First Thessalonians 5:19). We stop at the tabernacle veil too many times.

We have programmed our church services so tightly that we really don't leave room for the Holy Spirit. Oh, we might let God speak prophetically to us a little, but we get nervous if He tries to break out of our schedules. We can't let God out of the box too much because He can ruin everything.

At the same time, we still have our sign up. We still take people into our churches and show them the ovens where we used to bake bread. The ovens are all still in place and everything is there, but all you can find is crumbs from last year's visitation and the last great wave of revival our predecessors talked about. Now we are reduced to being shallow students of what we hope to experience some day. I'm constantly reading about revival, and God impressed upon me recently, "Son, you're reading about it because you don't yet have the experience to write about."

I am tired of reading about God's visitations of yesteryear. I want God to break out somewhere in my lifetime so that in the future my children can say, "I was there. I know; it's true." God has no grandchildren. Each generation must experience His presence. Recitation was never meant to take the place of visitation.

Compared to what God wants to do, *we're digging for crumbs in the carpet when He has hot loaves baking in the ovens of Heaven!* He is not the God of crumbs and lack. He is waiting just to dispense unending loaves of His life-giving presence, but our problem was described long ago by James the apostle, "...ye have not, because ye ask not" (Jas. 4:2).

We need to understand that what we have, where we are, and what we are doing is small compared to what He wants to do among and through us.

In the past, too many of us have been content to keep our faith contained within the four walls of our meeting halls and church buildings. Now God is calling us to extend our faith beyond to the boundaries of our cities and nation. In effect, we are literally expanding the "walls" of our spiritual churches when we go for our cities. It forces us to see ourselves as "the Church" in the city, one people under

God comprised of many congregations according to the first century pattern of the "city-church."

I believe God has stirred such a pent-up demand for His presence that in the "day of the Lord" (if His people will pursue His presence), the existing churches will not be able to handle the explosion of lost souls wanting to be saved. The modern Church is a caretaker or a maintenance organization at best, and a museum of what once was, at worst. Our greatest problem is that we've "stocked our shelves" with the wrong stuff. We offer the hungry our dusty shelves of bland, man-produced religious ritual that no one in his right mind is really hungry for! Empty religious ritual is as appetizing as "blue mashed potatoes" or some other unnatural concoction. If anybody could ever open a store that just dispenses Jesus, the hungry masses would come. Perhaps the reason we haven't stocked our services with the right stuff is because it doesn't come cheap.

The sad reality may be that most Christians in America don't have a real sense of the abiding presence of God because they refuse to clean up the clutter in their lives. And many of us who attempt to clear the clutter tend to get stuck in the logjam of legalism.

We want God to change the world. But *He cannot change the world until He can change us.* In our present state we are in no position to affect anything. But if we will submit to the Master Potter, He will make us—all of us—into what He needs us to be. He may remake the vessel of our flesh many times, but if we will submit to the Potter's touch, He can turn us into vessels of honor, power, and life.

Some of us seem to thrive on the momentary revelations of God when He wants us to press in for His secret things. He loves to honor the prayers of persistent pursuers like Moses, but He will actually stop our attempts to build monuments to partial and incomplete revelations of His glory—especially ones that we never paid for with our prayers and death on the altar of brokenness. We like things to come quickly, easily, and cheaply—microwave revival. God knows that such things never produce godly character in us.

It is time for the Church to truly embrace the cross of Jesus. Our hunger must propel us beyond the death of the flesh into the life and light of God's glory. It is the destiny of the Church of the living God. But it will only happen when we lay down the security of the "new covenant law" of religious practice and carefully controlled "supernatural" visitations for the apparent uncertainty and risk of living face-to-face with our supernatural God.

God doesn't want us to turn away from His glory so we can build pitiful monuments to a momentary revelation we never paid for with our tears. Salvation is a free gift, but God's glory will cost us everything. He wants us to press in and live in His perpetual habitation of glory. He wants us to be so saturated with His presence and glory that we carry His presence with us everywhere we go in this life. This may be the only way the unspeakable glory of God will find its way to the shopping malls, hair salons, and grocery stores of our nation.

This is the way God's glory is destined to cover the whole earth. *It has to start somewhere. Why not you? Why not me?* The fountains of flesh have to be broken up, as well as the windows of Heaven opened up, for the glory to gush out like a river and cover the earth.

And then all mankind will see…

GodChasers.network is the ministry of Tommy and Jeannie Tenney. Their heart's desire is to see the presence and power of God fall—not just in churches, but on cities and communities all over the world.

How to contact us:

By Mail:

> **GodChasers.network**
> **P.O. Box 3355**
> **Pineville, Louisiana 71361**
> **USA**

By Phone:

> Voice: 318.44CHASE (318.442.4273)
> Fax: 318.442.6884
> Orders: 888.433.3355

By Internet:

> E-mail: GodChaser@GodChasers.net
> Website: www.GodChasers.net

Run With Us!

Become a GodChasers.network Monthly Revival Partner

GodChasers are people whose hunger for Him compels them to run—not walk—towards a deeper and more meaningful relationship with the Almighty! For them, it isn't just a casual pursuit. Traditional Sundays and Wednesdays aren't enough—they need Him everyday, in every situation and circumstance, the good times and bad. Are you a GodChaser? Do you believe the body of Christ needs Revival? If my mandate of personal, National and International Revival is a message that resonates in your spirit, I want you to prayfully consider Running with us! Our Revival Partners fuel GodChasers.network to bring the message of unity and the pursuit of His presence around the world! And the results are incredible, yet humbling. As a Revival Partner, your monthly seed becomes the matches we use to set Revival fires around the globe.

For your monthly support of at least thirty dollars or more, I will send you free, personal fuel each month. This could be audio or videotapes of what I feel the Lord is saying that month. In addition, you will receive discounts on all of our ministry resources. Your Revival Partner status will automatically include you in invitation-only gatherings where I will minister in a more intimate setting.

I rely on our Revival Partners to intercede for the ministry in prayer and even minister with us at GodChaser gatherings around the country. I love to sow seed in peoples' lives and have learned that you can't out give God, He always multiplies the seed! If we give Him something to work with, there's no limit how many He can feed, or how many Revival fires can be started!

Will you run with us every month?

In Pursuit,

Tommy Tenney

Tommy Tenney

Become a Monthly Revival Partner by calling or writing to:

Tommy Tenney/GodChasers.network

P.O. Box 3355

Pineville, Louisiana 71361-3355

318.44CHASE (318.442.4273)

Other **God Chaser** Gift Books
Available Everywhere
God Chasers for Teens 0-7684-2153-5
God Chasers for Kids 0-7684-2165-9

For a complete list of our titles,
visit us at www.destinyimage.com
Send a request for a catalog to:

Destiny Image® Publishers, Inc.
P.O. Box 310
Shippensburg, PA 17257-0310